# Just Tuning My
# Air Guitar

## STORIES AND POEMS FROM
## THE ARKANSAS DELTA

*Clyde Allen Rodgers*

## CLYDE ALLEN RODGERS

PublishAmerica
Baltimore

First printing

ISBN: 1-4137-8468-2
PUBLISHED BY PUBLISHAMERICA, LLLP
www.publishamerica.com
Baltimore

Printed in the United States of America

## DEDICATION

*This collection is a compilation of a lifetime of work. I dedicate this book to my wife, Angela, who has encouraged me and inspired me as a writer; and to my grandsons, Courtney and Grayson. I also dedicate this collection of work to my English composition instructor, Mr. Jerry Gibbens, who is still teaching at Williams Baptist College in Walnut Ridge, Arkansas, and who is still inspiring students to be the best they can be.*

ACKNOWLEDGMENTS

*There are many people who have supported me in my writing over the years. I would like to thank some of the folks at East Arkansas Community College in Forrest City for their help and friendship. I gratefully acknowledge the support of Dr. Coy Grace, Jan Haven, Beth Loeb, and Debbie Wilkes. I would also like to acknowledge my fellow English instructors at EACC, Cathie Cline, Jeff Debuhr, and Jim McInturff, for their encouragement and support.*

# Just Tuning My
# Air Guitar

## Stories and Poems from
## the Arkansas Delta

# Just Tuning My Air Guitar

When I was just a kid and growing up out on the farm,
I'd play the air guitar. I guess it didn't do no harm.
I'll bet that every boy who's ever owned a radio
Has played the air guitar and been the star of his own show.

The mirror was my stage and was my audience as well.
I'd play my air guitar, and I could cast a mighty spell.
When Johnny Cash would sing a song like "Folsom Prison Blues,"
I'd grab my air guitar and try to dance out of my shoes.

The rock-a-billy sound was all I ever listened to,
And my old air guitar would go, "ba-DO-ba-DO-ba-DO."
But in between the songs I'd always do the strangest thing.
I'd tune my air guitar, and I mean every single string.

I'd take my air guitar, and I would sit down on the bed,
To see if it still matched up with the chords inside my head.
I'd tweak a key and pluck a string and listen to the sound.
I'd keep that up until some sense of harmony I'd found.

I don't know why I always thought that I should take the time
To tune that air guitar. I guess it's just a quirk of mine.
And many times since then I've found myself engaged in things
That seem about as ludicrous as tuning silent strings.

I wonder what this says about my personality.
Does it suggest an anal mind or creativity?
I want to understand me, but I won't get very far
Until I know the reasons why I tuned my air guitar.

*And the damsel was very fair, and cherished the king...*
                                                    *I Kings 1:4*

## Dancing Boy

King David was a man after God's own heart, the guys at the
   coffee shop would say.
They were mighty proud of their giant slayer; their would-be
   temple builder;
Their writer of pretty verses; their
Dancing Boy.

But his love life was all the talk in the mornings.
That first wife, King Saul's daughter, tried to rain
On his God-parade on the day that David brought
The Ark of the Lord into his brand-new capital city.
David was the Grand Marshal, and he danced in the streets
   with joy.
"My daddy never acted like that," the wife scoffed. "Get a grip,
   Dancing Boy!"
The coffee drinkers about died laughing at that whole affair.

He didn't have much luck with the next Mrs. David, either.
They kinda got off on the wrong foot.
It was a bloody affair.
He had her husband killed and later wished he hadn't.
The coffee shop got a little quite for a few days.
Everybody felt a bit uncomfortable.
They loved him, but this was no laughing matter.
Yet, they all agreed that he'd made a fine king.
But, buddy, that Dancing Boy sure could pick 'em.

In his old age, his body was frail and weak.
All those women had taken a powder.
The poor old fellow shivered in his bed, cold and alone.
His teeth chattered like maracas.
The coffee drinkers felt a little sorry for their Dancing Boy.
They hated to see him come to this sad end.

10

But the old king's sons got a bright idea.
They scoured the countryside and found a pretty young girl
And brought her to his bed.
"That ought to cheer up our Dancing Boy," the coffee drinkers said.
They thought the whole thing was pretty funny, though—
Old man like that, with that fine young thing in bed.
"That's our Dancing Boy! But, I doubt he can do her any good?"
They were a tough crowd, these coffee drinkers.

But how could they know?
How could they ever understand how she loved him so,
How she snuggled up to him and kept him warm in the night?
How could they know what it was like,
For her,
Lying there beside this gentle old fellow who could
Recite beautiful poetry in the night, in whispered tones,
And hold her to his scarred old chest,
And stroke her soft hair?
A young girl like that, in a man's world, can get some pretty
rough treatment, sometimes.

But Abishag just lay there in the arms of her
Dancing Boy,
And put her tiny feet around his, to keep them all cozy and warm,
And slept like a baby.

# Body Odor Blues

Since soap is cheap and water's free,
There is a thing that bothers me.
Why must I sit each day in class
And smell the other fellow's ass?

The world is filled with putrid smells,
Like sewage dumps and diaper pails.
I've emptied bedpans (what a chore).
I've wiped green vomit off the floor.

But these are smells I must endure;
For them, there is no simple cure.
But soap is cheap and water's free,
So body odor bothers me!

## To Woman

There is an emptiness in man.
He is bare walls and curtainless windows.
He is fire without warmth,
Earth without rain.

And that is why we wrap you in strong arms
And pull you to our chests
And touch you to our lips
And drink you.

That is why we long to hold you
And have your warmth envelop us.
We would press you into our souls
And make ourselves complete.

# Maybe So, but Maybe Not

Is autumn bleaker than the spring?
It's all in how you view the thing.
To bud more blessed than to rot?
Maybe so, but maybe not.

Sprinting youth or tottering age?
Unwritten lines or encumbered page?
Would I choose youth to be my lot?
Maybe so, but maybe not.

# I'm Only the Apple

I'm only the apple and innocent Eve,
Enticed by the serpent, was led to believe
That all would be well if she dared to partake.
Misguided to mischief, she made her mistake.

"You tricked me, Old Apple! You led me to shame!
And now I'm disgraced, and it's you who's to blame,"
Said Eve in her anger, while taking a bite.
Now I know that she knows that this is not right!

I'm only an apple. The serpent's to blame.
'Twas he who ensnared her and led her to shame.
And my only fault is just hanging around
And looking delightful and temptingly round.

But I must admit that I'm glad she came by
And took me and tasted. She has a good eye.
I'm sweeter than many; I longed for her bite.
Who cares if her tasting was wrong or was right?

## Entertaining Angels Unawares

I created an urban myth one night, and it has gone nationwide.
I picked up an angel named Jack, hitchhiking on I-55.
He was disguised as an old man, just as stodgy as he could be.
But all that getup was wasted on a smart guy like me.
He may just as well have worn his wings
And brought his halo and harp and other angel things.
You're probably thinking that I've lost my mind.
But the truth is, I pick up angels all the time.
This one smelled of month-old sweat and sour wine.
He climbed right in and started feeding me a line.
Angels, generally, are fine storytellers.
They lie like rugs, but they're pretty decent fellers.
I've always been a sucker for a good story,
And his were filled with guts and glory.
He'd fought in World War II, he said.
He'd left many a "goose-stepping bastard" dead.
He told me of all his travels, not a few.
And every single thing I shouldn't do
To bring me luck and happiness.
He said, "Don't do that and don't do this."
And he had one other thing to say—
Said he hadn't eaten at all that day.
Then he said, in a whining tone,
That he'd slept last night and all alone,
Huddled up under an overpass,
Beneath a canopy of grass.
Angels shouldn't have to live like that.
They can pull rabbits out of a hat,
And make themselves soft, furry beds
With fluffy pillows for their heads.
He said, if he had money, he'd buy me gas.
He made me the offer, and I hadn't even asked.
(Angels say things to put me to the test.
I hate that, but they know best.)
I told him we'd just let that pass.

I was on my way to the state pen to teach an English class.
That's another smart thing I do.
Most convicts, you know, are angels, too.
They write interesting essays, full of grammar mistakes,
About how to bake hacksaw blades into birthday cakes.
I took Old Jack to a motel and put him up for the night.
It cost me twenty bucks, but that was all right.
I also gave him some money for food.
He winked and said, "I appreciate it, dude!"
(As if he didn't know my name.)
Let me tell you, angels know everything.
He gave me a stinky hug, and I hugged him back.
And I said, "Well, good luck. See you later, Jack."
I think he knew I was on to his game,
So I asked him something that sounded really lame.
"Do you believe in angels?" I asked.
Said he'd heard lots of stories in the past,
And he reckoned they might be true.
"Well," I said, "you've been one to me, and I've been one to you."
If you were shucking oysters by the seaside,
Wouldn't you check each one to see if a pearl's inside?
I would, and I think you would, too.
Entertaining angels is a smart thing to do.

# To Courtney, My Grandson

Since my mortality may not await your manhood,
I cannot delay, until you're a man, to be understood.
I must tell you now.
You were only seven and may not now remember
the trip we made to the fair, on a fall Sunday,
and the ride we rode together.

At first you rode the Kiddie Scrambler.
It was a slow, methodic ambler.
And I just stood there on the side
And watched you as you made your ride.

Bravado is, at times, so lame.
The ride was slow and smooth and tame,
like metered verse—a calm affair.
You stuck both hands into the air.

You were a showboat, unabashed.
I smiled and waved each time you passed.

But something about the way you behaved bothered me,
inside.
I knew that life is not always metered rhyme.
Sometimes, it's free verse and can really be a jolting ride.
It can jerk you around and slam you against the side.
It can be a frightening time, and cockiness is not always a good quality.
Suddenly, I felt compelled, and I don't know why,
to take you for a roller coaster ride.
You barely met the minimum height required.

We stood long in the line,

together.

And we could hear the rumbling din above our heads.
"It goes really fast," you said.
And the fear in your eyes made me feel guilty,
so I gave you the perfect out.
"We don't have to ride," I said.
This, I thought, is not what fun's about.

"How long does it last, Pappy?" you asked.
I timed the car as it made its run,
and it took two snail-like minutes of tedious time.
I took your little hand in mine.
"Let's not ride," I begged.

But you would not turn back.

We loaded into the car and began our ride, creeping skyward,
ever closer to the dropping-off place.
And I looked at your face.
I saw a frightened grimace there, out of place, I thought, on a
      seven-year-old.
"It's not so bad, see there?"
I said, hoping to erase the pitiful stare.

"But when we get to the top, it will be," you said.

I wished we had not come.
You understood too much of dread, I thought,
and fear.
I should not have ever brought you here.
I felt cruel for having put you to the test.
When we reached the top, you averted your eyes
and turned your shoulder to the front,
like one walking into the wind,
like a Rebel soldier in Pickett's fight.
And you gripped the bar with all your might.

Your eyes were toward, but not on, me.

You faced the coming doom alone.

As we plunged downward, you held on so tight, grimly
      determined to make this fight
for life and limb and honor and victory over fright. When it was
      over and we stepped out,
there was no smugness on your face,
But a look,
bone-tired,
and of
relief.

You were clothed in valor, it seemed to me.

And I knew that you would be all right. And though I might not live
to see you grown, I knew, that day, that I'd been shown the man
that you'd grow to be. I had been allowed to see the seed.
I guess that met some need
in me.

You had some steel inside your soul
and understood the greater whole,
and knew that there's a darker dread
and gave no ground to fear. Instead,
you rode the wild, chaotic line,
and gave your Pappy peace of mind.

## The Student

Like an enthusiast in an art gallery,
I stand in awe of you,
And I am amazed at the delicacy
Of every detail—

The flush of your cheeks;
The way the light dances off your hair;
The depth of color in your eyes;
The curve of your body;
These all flood my senses. I stammer,
In search of fitting words to respond.

Yet, I know that this art goes far beyond my poor powers
Of observation. For each time I look,
I see a brush stroke, a reflection of light,
A shadow, or a hue
I had not noticed before.

And I detest the blindness
That has robbed me of this pleasure
Until now.

# Agamemnon Re-Butchered

Agamemnon, what a dummy!
Got a knife stuck in his tummy
When he came home from the battle,
Armor rusty, sword a-rattle.

Clytemnestra was there waiting,
His return anticipating,
And he came home, not suspecting
That her mind was on dissecting.

You may wonder why this mean wife
Was so quick to stick her keen knife
In the entrails of her warrior.
What had he done to annoy her?

Well, we must go back a little,
In the past, to solve the riddle,
To the day of his departing,
When the war was only starting.

Agie's men were armed and ready.
All they needed was a steady
Breeze to fill their sails with power,
But the wind god's mood was sour.

While they sat there, void of motion,
Agamemnon got the notion
That to put things back in order
He must sacrifice his daughter.

Then the wind god's mood was happy!
And the winds became quite snappy!
There were cheers from all the fellows
As the wind blew like a bellows.

When he came home from the battle,
Armor rusty, sword a-rattle,
Shouts of praise were loudly ringing,
But Cassandra started singing.

"Oh, this will be a day of sorrow!
There will be no bright tomorrow
For the hero of the battle."
Agie jeered, "Such foolish prattle!"

So, he stepped out on the scarlet
Rug provided by the harlot.
And, he strutted, filled with glory,
To a death scene, red and gory.

Agamemnon, what a dummy!
Got a knife stuck in his tummy
When he came home from the battle,
Armor rusty, sword a-rattle.

# Teaching Behind the Wire

The wire has barbs as sharp as fangs
To slice the flesh and bone
Of any man who dares to try
To leave and go back home.

Who are these men behind the wire?
What evil fiends are they?
What dreadful dangers do they pose?
Why are they locked away?

Are these men martyrs, saints, or gods
Unjustly locked away,
Or are they vile and vicious brutes
Who must be made to pay?

They've written papers for my class.
I've taught them what I can,
Of writing (that most precious art
that gives a voice to man).

They've shared with me their deepest thoughts.
They've bared their souls to me.
I've seen another side of them
That many cannot see.

Their minds are sharp; their souls, intact.
And they still have that spark
Of men who, in God's image, shine
A light into the dark.

And some have children whom they miss
And love, as I love mine.
And some have wives or sweethearts whom
They think of all the time.

They've treated me with great respect
And worked so tirelessly.
I hope they've learned a tenth as much
As they have taught to me.

I've learned that simple platitudes
Like "throw away the key"
Reflect the silly shallowness
Of our society.

I've learned that strands of razor wire,
Coiled on a granite wall,
Cannot confine the human mind
Or make the spirit fall.

These men have taught me just how strong
That I, myself, can be.
Though I be bound, both hand and foot,
My spirit can be free.

They are not fiends, nor are they saints.
These men are simply men
Who took their fall and dusted off
And stood upright again.

They've chosen to redeem the time
By using it to learn.
By doing that, they may rebuild
Some bridges they had burned.

For I have seen them dare to dream
And daringly aspire
To break the walls of darkness down—
These men behind the wire.

# Your Gown of Light Blue

As you lie here beside me, asleep on your pillow,
I look at those soft lips that I love to kiss,
And I think of the passion that we just shared together,
And I know that no woman was ever loved more than this.

(Chorus)
*Sleeping beside me in your gown of light blue,*
*You awaken my senses, my passion renew.*
*And, if this is what love is, then I must confess—*
*There has never been a woman who was loved more than this.*

Your lips are as soft as the petals of roses.
Your hair is as shiny as grass touched with dew.
The blue gown you're wearing is as sheer as the moonlight
That shines in and highlights the perfection that's you.

But youth is a flower that blooms in the springtime,
Matures in the summer, but fades in the fall.
I know you must wonder, when your youth has faded,
If I will still love you or want you at all.

Well, there is a beauty that's deep down inside you
That has captured my heart and imprisoned my soul,
And my love will last through the passing of seasons,
And I will still love you, even as we grow old.

## The Pioneers

They left crowded cities and played-out farmlands.
They came by ox cart and prairie schooner.
They rode on horseback and in rickety wagons.
They trudged on toward the setting sun,
Ever westward.

They left many precious keepsakes behind.
Others, they discarded along wagon trails:
Grandfather clocks, chests of drawers,
And many a bride's dowry,
Too heavy or too cumbersome for the journey,
Ever westward.

They brought their axes and their breaking plows.
They brought their muskets and their powder horns:
Tools with which to carve out a home in the wilderness,
Tools with which to provide bread and meat for the table.
They pushed on, along dim and dangerous trails,
Ever westward.

Milch cows and plow mules, led by barefoot boys;
Fair-skinned girls in homespun dresses and faded bonnets;
Sad-eyed women who looked much older than their years;
Men with dark and leathery faces; all plodded on,
Ever westward.

They were driven westward by a dream,
A dream of owning their own land,
Of being independent and free.
It was do or die, in stark and literal terms.
There would be no turning back, just
Ever westward.

They cast their eyes over a new land
And picked out their own spot of earth.

They laid the axe to the root of the tree
And cleared the land for farming.
From the logs, they raised up crude cabins,
And, in them, they raised up a generation of Americans, looking
Ever westward.

# Carpe Winkum

The boldest wasp I ever saw
Attended class at Ouachita.
He owned a condo on the eave
Outside our classroom, I believe.
And he would listen every day
To all my teacher had to say.
The teacher's name was Johnny Wink.
The wasp would listen, pause, and think.

Creative Writing was the course.
And John would lecture with such force.
*"Oh, Carpe Diem!"* he would shout.
And up he'd jump and prance about
As if the things he had to say
Were road maps to a better way
To live this nanosecond life.
His words would cut me like a knife.

*"Out!—Out! Brief candle! Seize the day!*
*Our lives are short! They slip away!*
*Oh, dare to do, while there's still time!*
*Now write a poem. Make it rhyme."*
I listened to the things he said.
I pondered them inside my head,
And thought, "He's got it going on.
I know he'd never steer us wrong."

The girl who sat in front of me
Was just as lovely as could be.
Her hair was blonde; her eyes were blue.
She glistened like the morning dew.
She smelled like apples in the hay.
I absolutely loved the way
She tossed her head and pooched her lips
And stroked them with her fingertips.

So, I determined, then and there,
To cast aside my every care
And tell this beauty how I felt.
Perhaps, I thought, her heart would melt,
And she'd be mine, to have and hold.
"Oh, Carpe Diem!" I'd been told.
So, I leaned up to make my move.
The time was right! I had my groove!

Just then the wasp came flying in
And landed on her dimpled chin.
Straight up shot she and danced around.
Her scream was such a chilling sound.
As smooth as silk, Ol' Wink arose.
(The wasp had flown up to her nose.)
*"I'm in control. No need to fear."*
(The wasp then shifted to her ear.)

He took a paper in his hand.
The wasp jumped on at his command.
He took him to the windowsill.
The wasp flew off. He'd had his fill.
My chance was gone. The moment passed,
And she was gone out of my grasp.
The wasp got nectar. I got dregs.
And he flew home to lick his legs.

# The Giant Baby Visits the House of Bay and Becomes the Envy of the High and Mighty

*(Observations on a visit from my college instructor,
my mentor, and my friend, Dr. Johnny Wink)*

Old Plato must have found some joy
in mentoring the golden boy.
But Aristotle couldn't blend
a margarita for his friend.

And, Major Nelson, after all,
had Jeannie at his beck and call.
The Giant Baby had a brace
of genies in that lovely place
who waited on his every need.
He is a lucky child indeed.

And oh how Oprah loves to chat.
But some have found her stale and flat.
But on his visit a' chez Bay,
the Giant Baby talked away.
They hung on every single word
as if they fed on what they heard.

Bill Hickok was a man of fame,
and poker was his favorite game.
We know the end of that affair.
A bullet parted Hickok's hair.
The Giant Baby got to play
while he was at the House of Bay.
Though losing to him was a pain,
they put no bullet in his brain.

King Solomon of ancient times
had scores of lovely concubines.

He never had to sleep alone.
He thought he had it going on.
The Giant Baby went to bed.
He thought he was alone. Instead,
he found there, to his great surprise,
a dark-haired beauty with such eyes
as most men only see in dreams.
The Baby's life is charmed, it seems.
Her legs were long; her body, sleek.
She didn't make a sound or speak.
She tiptoed in on puppy feet
and lay beside his bed to sleep.

So, fame and fortune have their place.
They're valued by the human race.
But they cannot be priced above
the boon of deep respect and love.

## A Granule of Truth

The poet walks among the ghosts,
Down eerie paths and wanton.
Surrounded by the shadowy hosts,
He fears he has become one.

Like Morely's oyster, he's apart,
Though in a crowded seabed.
The rest see not his sand-scored heart,
Their Eden's unmolested.

He bears the brunt of borrowed pain
And mourns for mystic masses.
He wets his cheeks with salty rain.
But, noticeless, he passes.

The tortured oyster makes a pearl
That no one may discover.
Cassandra cried (that poor sad girl)
But could not save her lover.

The poet, ghostlike, plods along,
Down life's most lonely hollows,
And softly sings his poet's song
And hopes that someone follows.

## To Angela, My Eve

The boughs of Eden's splendid trees
Sagged low with fruit of perfect hue,
And all of nature strained to please
The god-man it owed homage to.

But lost in his own discontent,
Poor Adam wandered hill and dell
And grieved the sad predicament
That turned his Eden into hell.

Then God looked down and saw his plight
And knew His work was incomplete.
God gave him Eve to make things right.
He woke to find her at his feet.

Both joy and pain would come their way,
But with this woman in his life,
He'd never see a lonely day.
He'd found his Eden in his wife.

Before you came to walk with me,
To be my soul mate and my wife,
No fruits of Eden could I see,
But you brought Eden to my life.

# Living Poetry

There are those who write poems
And those who live them.
I want to do both if I can.

————————————

My pappy couldn't read or write,
But his life was a simile
That could cut like a knife.

One fall Sunday we rode the farm roads
In his old pickup. He stopped and, without a word,
Got out and climbed up into the bed of the truck.

I followed him. He picked me up and hoisted me
Up over his head and put me atop his shoulders.
He turned slowly, around and around.

The cotton was ready for harvest.
It was a breath-taking sight,
Banks of snow, so beautifully white.

"Thangs looks differnt fum up here,"
He said. And when he set me down,
There was a poem welling up in his eyes.

————————————

I used to do carpentry work
To supplement my teacher's pay.
A little old lady called me one day.

"Can you hang wallpaper?" she asked.
I told her that I could.
Then she asked, "Can you do it good?"

We stood in her bathroom, looking
At the world's worst wallpapering job. The pieces
Were starkly unaligned and comically unattached.

"Me and my late husband done this job," she said.
"We didn't know what we was doing a-tall.
I fussed at him, and he fussed back and made me bawl."

"He never could stand to see me cry,
So he got down and hugged me and said,
'Let's go in the kitchen and eat something sweet.'"

"That's what he always said when we'd fuss.
'Let's go eat something sweet'
And we would, and then everything would be good."

I looked at her face, and I saw a poem written there.
I took her gnarled, arthritic little hand in mine,
And we wept together over the death of the poet.

————————————————

There are those who write poems
And those who live them.
I want to do both if I can.

# The Bane Narcissus: Oh, the Humanity!

I once had a student who seemed to be smart.
The Comp I assignments he turned in were art.
But something about them just struck me as odd.
His essays suggested he thought he was God.

To shield his identity, I'll call him Lee.
And making "Lee" rhyme will be easy for me.
(Just try it with "Damian"; then you will see
How clever I am to be calling him Lee.)

He dotted his "I's" and he crossed all his "T's."
He toiled like a Trojan his teacher to please.
Most teachers would kill for a student like Lee,
But, frankly, his essays were heinous to me.

Now, self-adoration is not a bad thing,
Unless it is labored and in the extreme.
For instance, one paper he turned in to me
Was titled "How Wonderful Just To Be Lee."

His diction was pithy; his syntax, sublime.
And his sense of timing could stop on a dime.
His theme on description was titled "Here's Me."
Comparison/Contrast inspired "Why Not Lee?"

I grew to detest him, in spite of his flair.
And by mid-semester, I'd pulled out my hair.
Just reading his essays would fill me with rage,
This loathsome Lee business, just page upon page.

Then, all of a sudden (Oh, how could it be!),
When I got to class, there was NO sign of Lee.
I thought it was over! Narcissus, no more!
But then, to my doom, came a knock at my door.

"I just got a call from a student of yours.
He's having some problems now, but he assures,
He wants to return and continue your class.
He asked me to ask you if he can still pass.

"His problems are medical. He's at the Med.
I know you could flunk him, but I think, instead,
You OUGHT to work WITH him. He seems a nice guy."
At that point, the dean had a tear in his eye.

I sat there befuddled, my tail 'tween my legs.
Dean Bridges can look so forlorn when he begs.
Well, Oh, the humanity! Oh, the dark mood!
A curse on your houses! Oh, vain attitude!

With Lee in my future, I hated my life.
To deal with the trauma, I needed my wife.
Her sweet disposition has always been such
That problems will vanish away at her touch.

The fact that she works at the Med says that she
Is more dedicated than she has to be.
The work is demanding, and only the strong,
Most constant of nurses endure there for long.

No problem from work takes the smile from her face.
There's never a frown, no, not even a trace.
I once was that way, in my life before Lee,
Before his dread poison infiltrated me

I drove home and waited for her to walk in,
And carefully pondered just how to begin.
If she could but grasp my abhorrence of Lee,
Could her sweet demeanor help pacify on me?

But, as Fate would have it (Can't Fate be a slut?),
She came through the door like a camel in rut,
Just grunting and snorting and having a fit.
She threw down her stethoscope, shouting, "I QUIT!"

It seems that a patient they'd brought in that day
Had got on her nerves in the worst kind of way.
She said he was constantly needing a nurse.
She added, "Just trust me; the story gets worse."

She said, when he'd ring, she would run right on down
And find him as nude as the eyes of a clown,
And there'd be his penis, as hard as a gem.
She said that she couldn't bear looking at him.

She said she would tell him to pull up the sheet.
And then he would pull it up, ever so neat.
And he would say laughingly, "Look! It's a tent!"
And that was how all of her day had been spent.

I listened intently, with nothing to say,
As she went on telling about her bad day.
But I was as shocked as a fellow could be
When, all of a sudden, I heard her say "Lee."

"Do you mean to tell me this puke's name is Lee?"
I asked, and she nodded and said, "Yessiree!"
I said, "He's my student!" And she said, "Egad!"
I asked her what sort of a problem he had.

Well, THAT, she informed me, I would not believe.
She said that the doctors had had to retrieve
A dildo, ensconced in the fusty confines
Of that part of Lee where the sun never shines.

He'd called 911 in a horrible state
And cried, "Hurry up, or you may be too late!
I'm bleeding profusely! I fear I will die!
I have an appliance up my nether eye!"

The doctors released him, and Lee was sent home.
He's sitting in class on a donut of foam.
He's writing away, just as calm as can be.
His essay's entitled "It Hurts to Love Lee."

Narcissus! Narcissus! Just look what you've done!
You've set an example, you son of a gun!
You looked in the water and found your true love.
Now, take out your dildo and give it a shove!

# Pappy's Poem to Grayson

I guess that it's a trick of fate
That grandsons come around so late
In pappys' lives. It seems a shame.
We must accept it just the same.

So, by the time that you were born,
Your pappy's shoes were old and worn.
He'd had the time to find a wife
To walk beside through his life.

He'd seen a daughter come of age
And start to write her own life's page.
To him she gave a special gift
That gave his latter steps a lift.

Our time together on this earth
Will be of such a narrow girth.
Your pappy has but autumn years
To share your laughter and your tears.

I picked you up at school one day.
And all the kids were hard at play.
But you had somehow misbehaved.
That scene is in my memory saved.

It seemed an awful price to pay.
I never will forget the way
You looked there in that timeout chair.
It broke my heart to see you there.

Though lots of time has passed us by,
I still remember with a sigh
You sitting in that lonely space,
That look of sadness on your face.

A tear welled up in Pappy's eye.
I could not let you see me cry.

My Mustang was your favorite car,
And folks could hear you, near and far,
When I'd put on your favorite song,
And you'd so loudly sing along.

"A Man of Sorrows" was the tune,
And, buster, you could really croon.
"...of constant saw-wock," you would sing.
And you could make that fiddle ring.

You'd saw the air with all your might
And hold that fiddle up just right
And stomp your foot to mark the beat.
To watch you was a special treat.

Since you performed on my behalf,
I could not let you see me laugh.

We used to play a deadly game,
But I don't think it had a name.
The crocodile would lie in wait
And plan the "mud-knot's" awful fate.

*While sitting in my favorite chair,*
*I am the croc! I'm in my lair!*
*The mud-knot comes a strolling by*
*And looks as sweet as pumpkin pie!*

*As quick as lightning, I attack!*
*The frightened mud-knot's fighting back!*
*I try so hard to take a bite!*
*The mud-knot makes it out all right.*
You'd laugh so hard and come right back
And sometimes give me such a whack
that it would almost take my breath.
You'd try to beat that croc to death.

The game was yours and mine alone.
I could not let you hear me groan.

Such mysteries the future holds.
We're walking blind as time unfolds.
But these few things I know for sure:
My love for you is clean and pure.

And up the path lie joy and pain.
And we won't come this way again.
But one day you will read these lines,
And you'll remember all the times

That I have shared your pain and joy
And know that Pappy loved his boy.

# The Smell of Horses I Never Rode

It's when I stop at one of those modern day
serviceless service stations
to fill the bottomless pit of my own tank
with that gasoline, gasoline
refined from that blood-soaked Arab oil,
and wash my own windshield
(which shields me from the wind and the rain),
that I sometimes long to be shielded also from the pain
of having to go inside and pay.

But it's not the wad of dirty bills with which I am about to part
that hurts my silly heart.
It's the dull-eyed, cell-phone-talking,
don't-mess-with-me-attitude-having cashier
that I fear.

And I miss the smell of horses I never rode,
and I think, "God, I hate the twenty-first century."

# They Caught the BTK

They caught him today,
The fabled BTK.
Someone said, "It's no surprise,
For I could see it in his eyes."

He was a dogcatcher
And a victim fetcher.
Got by for thirty years.
Left a trail of tears.

Reckon why he'd do such a thing?
From whence did all the anger spring?
They interviewed a screwed-up guy about thirty.
He'd watched the man get down and dirty,

Twenty years ago, with his mother.
Said he's now on drugs of some sort or other.
"BTK screwed up my life," he said.
"I wanna see him good and freaking dead.

He knocked on our door one night.
I let him in. That wasn't right.
And, me, I'm just a junky,
All tattooed up and funky."

The hate and anger floating 'round.
They make a stark and screechy sound.
They make a stark and screechy sound.
The hate and anger floating 'round.

# The Homeless Woman in the Park

I saw her in the park today.
She hobbled as she made her way.
She sat beside me on the bench.
I barely could endure the stench.

The homeless hag was dressed in rags.
Her worldly treasures, crammed in bags,
She gently placed between her feet.
She smiled and whispered, "Ain't life sweet."

I gave no answer, just a nod.
She said, "You know, I'm blessed of God."
"That's good," I said and turned away.
She said, "Ain't it a lovely day?"

"Do you want money?" I inquired.
"To tell the truth, I'm really tired,
And I don't want to play your game.
But, here's a dollar, just the same."

She brushed the dollar bill away,
And said, "I'll pray for you today."
So, I got up and walked away.

# Uncle Rhymes

Every parent on the Bolandsville Plantation despised Red Connor, that is, all except my mama. She had a soft spot in her heart for all underdogs, and Red certainly was a member of that breed. His real name was Philip, but no one called him that except Mrs. Connor and Mama.

Daddy simply detested Red and all three of his bothers. "You stay away from those Connor boys!" Daddy must have said that to me a thousand times.

Being grown now, with children of my own, I guess I can't blame Daddy all that much. There is some truth to, "Birds of a feather flock together." I wouldn't want my daughters hanging around those boys. That's for sure. They could be a bad influence, to say the least. For one thing, those boys were lazy with a capital L. Back in those days, all the kids on the place had to chop and pick cotton during school vacation, all except the Connor boys. Odie Connor, the father and head of the clan, couldn't get his boys to do a lick of work. Lamont, Jinks, Rayford, and Red would sit on their front porch, play their guitars, sing Johnny Cash and George Jones songs, and watch the rest of us sweat when we were working in the field beside their house. Sometimes, but only rarely, Red would come out to the field and pick a boll or two and put the cotton into my sack. He'd be singing the whole time, but he sure didn't do any sweating. My daddy had only one measuring stick to size up the worth of a man. If he wouldn't work, he wasn't "worth a damn." So, according to Daddy, Red wasn't worth a damn.

But that is only one of the many reasons I was forbidden to associate with Red Connor. Red only came to school when he felt like it, and he got a whipping just about every day that he did attend. He

47

could curse better than anyone I knew. He and his brothers drove Odie's car ninety miles per hour down gravel roads, and they all drank like fish. If they couldn't afford store-bought whisky, they'd drink moonshine or Dr. Somebody's (I forget whose exactly) Elixir.

To be honest, my daddy's fears were not unfounded. Red did teach me a lot about vice. He talked me into smoking my first cigarette, drinking my first beer, and buying my first girlie magazine. In addition, he told me my first dirty joke (which involved a little fellow by the name of Johnny Pokerfaster), and he also showed me what good use those girlie magazines could be put to, if you know what I mean.

But, the fact is, Red Connor was witty and pure fun to be around. He had a brilliant mind and a shrewd sense of humor. Now, that is an unbeatable combination, and that is what endeared him to my mother. Red's favorite pastime was making people laugh, and Mama was an easy mark. She had had a difficult life. Daddy was a poor-as-dirt sharecropper. Mama had to do a lot of really hard fieldwork in her life, and she had had four kids by the time she was twenty-four. And, in spite of Daddy's obvious virility, he seldom showed her the tenderness that I thought she needed so badly. That was just not his way. But, in spite of all the hardships, Mama always looked for things to laugh about. Red was for her a godsend.

Of all his talents, the one that made me love Red the most was his uncanny ability to uncle rhyme. It all started one afternoon in our living room. Daddy was at work and Red knew it, so he came over to watch a Tarzan movie that was going to air on T.V. that afternoon. Red, Mama, and I loved Tarzan movies, and Mama had popped us some popcorn and made a pitcher of tea for the occasion. About midway through the movie, Tarzan was in quite a jam. Two white hunters were chasing him through the jungle, shooting at him. But, as usual, they had bitten off more than they could chew when they decided to mess with Tarzan. He led them right to a lion pit and they unceremoniously fell in. There were two lions in the pit, a big one and a little one. When the two white hunters hit the ground with a plop in front of them, the little lion looked up at the big lion and said, "Arr-raaar."

Neither Mama nor I understood lion lingo, but Red thought he did. He piped in an interpretation. In a really authentic-sounding

British accent, Red said, "This is enough for dinnah and suppah, Uncle Huppah."

God only knows why Mama and I thought that was so funny. It just was. We laughed, non-stop, for at least an hour. Red loved it. This was the thing he was good at, and he knew it.

After that day, uncle rhymes became Red's forte. But Red understood all about comic timing. He never overdid the thing. He would only uncle rhyme on rare occasions and at the most opportune times. As a result, uncle rhyming never became old hat.

Mama developed ovarian cancer in 1961, at the age of thirty-eight. I was twelve years old. She was operated on one Tuesday and died the following Friday. A big part of me died that day, too. The light had gone from my life, I felt. Neighbors filled the house, bringing food, paying their respects. Everybody on the place loved my mother, and the house was filled with the sounds of grief. It was more than I could bear. I went to my room to grieve in solitude. I sat on my bed in utter despair. I was alone in the world, I thought. Then the door cracked open, and Red peeped in.

"Can I come in for a minute?" he asked.

He sat down on the bed beside me. I could tell that he had been crying too. We sat there for a long time in total silence. Finally, Red patted my knee and said, "You'll get through it, Uncle Pruitt."

I looked up at Red and smiled, and he gave me a big hug. We just held on to each other and cried for a long time. Nothing else was said. Nothing else needed to be said.

From that day on, Red Connor assumed the awesome responsibility of being my savior. He determined in his heart that he would keep me alive and not let my sadness overwhelm me.

My daddy never did get to liking Red, but he finally just gave up on keeping us apart. Red became my constant companion, my right-hand trigger-man. And whenever he sensed that I was sinking into the abyss, he would try to pull me out by making me laugh or getting me to think about something else. Uncle rhyming was but one of the arrows in his quiver. He had plenty more.

A carnival came to Lepanto every fall. It was a good way for the hustlers to relieve the sharecroppers of some of their hard-earned money, and it was a nice little reward for us kids. When it came in the fall of '61, I had no intention of going, but Red insisted. The first thing

49

we did was fill up on carnival food and drink. There were so many exotic delights from which to choose that it was hard to decide which ones to buy. We finally settled on funnel cakes and lime sno-cones. I was soon to find out what a deadly combination that could be.

Red wanted to ride all the scariest rides. The biggest and baddest was the Roundup. It was this huge, round metal platform encircled by a metal fence. The whole contraption was suspended in the middle by the axle of some sort of giant turbo-powered engine that would spin the platform at an incredible speed. There was no need for safety belts, we were told, because the centrifugal force would pin the rider's back to the wire fence once the thing picked up some speed. That was an understatement. Once the thing got going good, my cheeks were flopping against my ear lobes and I couldn't move a muscle. Red, pinned beside me, was screaming his head off. He was terrified.

Then he screamed, "I'm fixin' to puke, Uncle Luke!"

No sooner had he said that when a two-fisted glob of green, wet dough ejected from his mouth, shot out about three feet, hovered in midair, and then came hurling back, hitting me squarely in the face. I could have killed him. But, I'll have to admit, it was pretty damned funny then, and it still is now when I think about it.

The first time I ever went on a date with a girl, it was a double date. Red talked Odie out of his car and we took out the Witherspoon twins, Zelda and Nelda. Everybody just called the girls "Z" and "N." Red arranged the whole thing. Z and N had no rivals on the farm when it came to experience. Red and I both were newcomers at this game. That night, Red found his manhood, or so he later claimed. We parked on the bridge just past the gin. Red took N for "a little walk." Z and I had the backseat, a venue with which Z seemed quite familiar. As it turned out, Z's experience failed to compensate for my lack of it, and the whole episode turned out to be a disaster. Just like the undertaker's daughter in The Godfather movie, "I kept my honor."

After we took them home and started for Odie's to return the car, Red looked over at me and asked, "Did you do her, Uncle Brewer?"

We walked to my house, and Red spent the night with me. We didn't sleep a wink. About the time I would be about to doze off, Red would ask, "Did you do her, Uncle Brewer?" and I would bust out laughing. Daddy kept hollering from his bedroom for us to pipe down, but Red wouldn't have any of it. I had to keep putting my pillow over my face to stifle the laughter so Daddy wouldn't yell at me. But every time I would get control and take the pillow off my face, Red would be waiting to waylay me.

"Did you top her, Uncle Hopper?"

"Did you hump her, Uncle Thumper?"

"Did you nail her, Uncle Taylor?"

"Did you poke her, Uncle Stoker?"

Each time, back under the pillow I would go. He kept it up all night.

Red quit school in the tenth grade. He was drinking a lot by then and had had a few brushes with the law. I was involved with school and a steady girlfriend and lots of other things. Red and I gradually drifted apart. I got out of school, got a job, got married, and started a family. My wife and I moved to Jonesboro to be near my work. I seldom saw Red Connor in those days. Then came college. I was off to Arkadelphia to attend Ouachita Baptist University. After graduation, I returned to Lepanto to teach high school English. I looked Red up and invited him over for dinner, but he failed to show up. As the years passed, I would see him occasionally on the street or in a store, and we would talk about old times.

In the summer of 1984, the chief of police asked me if I would work through the summer at the city jail as the night shift radio dispatcher. I agreed. One of my responsibilities was to check on any prisoners in the jail about every thirty minutes or so. We seldom had any prisoners. But then one night, when I arrived at the station, the day dispatcher informed me that we did, indeed, have a prisoner, that he was a troublesome sort, and that I had better keep a close eye on him.

When I made my first rounds, the one and only Red Connor was the guy sitting on that cot, behind those bars.

"Red, what are you doing in here?"

He had been sitting with his face in his hands, feeling mighty poorly, it appeared. But, at the sound of my voice, he perked up and smiled that old "Red" smile. He stood up, walked over to the bars, and said, "They threw me in jail, Uncle Dale."

I called the chief and promised to pay Red's bail. I took him to his mother's house in the squad car. Out of habit, Red started to get into the backseat.

51

"Get up front with me, Red," I said.

As I drove down Main Street, Red asked if he could turn on the lights and siren. I told him to go ahead. Of course, everyone on the street looked up to see what the emergency was. Red waved and hollered at everyone.

"This is so cool, Uncle Buell."

As he was getting out of the car, he looked me right in the eyes and asked me, "Are you staying happy these days, Bud?"

"Yes, Red, I am," I said.

"Good." Then he thanked me for getting him out of jail and went into the house.

Not long after that, Red got married. He married my cousin, in fact. My uncle wasn't too happy about it. The marriage went downhill fast. Glenda went home and filed for divorce. Red was brokenhearted. I went to see him. He was sitting on his mother's porch, drunker than Cooter Brown. I sat with him all afternoon. He cried a lot. I just tried to be a good listener and a good shoulder for him to cry on. I wanted to say, "You'll get through it, Uncle Pruitt," but I didn't feel worthy somehow.

Red drank too much Dr. Somebody's, I suppose. In 1986, he developed a serious stomach ulcer. His condition deteriorated rapidly. The doctors did what they could, but it was no use. I went to see him in the hospital. He was lying there with tubes stuck everywhere. I didn't think he was awake, and I wasn't going to disturb him. But, his eyes opened and he looked up and saw me standing there beside his bed. I took his hand and asked, "How are you feeling, old friend?"

He made a feeble attempt to produce that old "Red" smile and whispered something. I couldn't understand him, so I leaned in and put my ear right next to his mouth.

"Well, it's about over, Uncle Grover," he whispered.

I sat with him all night. He slept most of the time. And when he was awake, he was out of his head a good deal of the time. During one of his good spells, he told me to not let his death make me unhappy. He said he had been worrying about that. I told him not to worry and that I would be ok.

Red died the next day. I have thought about him many times in the years since his death. I have come to realize how much I am in his debt. When Mama died, Daddy let my sisters and me choose the epitaph to be etched on her tombstone. We chose "She was the sunshine of our home." Without her, there was a lot gloom and darkness in my life. Red Connor was the occasional and blessed beam of light. I owe him my life.

For all his talent, I think of Red always when I read Thomas Grey's poem, "Elegy Written in a Country Churchyard." "Full many a flower is born to blush unseen, and waste its sweetness on the desert air."

With his sharp mind and quick wit, with his spacious and kind heart, what potential Red Connor might have had if the world could have seen him as I saw him. He might have been a great poet, and he certainly could have been a great humanitarian. He could have helped the whole world to be a little brighter place. I was the lucky one. He was my own personal poet. I miss him, and I could use a good uncle rhyme right now.

# My Uncle Jack

When I was a kid growing up in the Arkansas Delta, most everybody knew that a surefire way for a fellow to get an ass whipping was to mess with William Jasper Mize, my Uncle Jack. He was my mother's older brother. He also was a sharecropper and a part-time city deputy in Lepanto, Arkansas. Most importantly, to me at least, he was also the toughest man in Poinsett County. Everybody who knew Jack knew that to be a fact. Some who didn't know him learned that truth the hard way—by getting their asses whipped. I'll have to admit that, at the tender age of twelve, I was awfully proud of my Uncle Jack. I was even cocky about it, I suppose. After all, he was a legend.

Being the son of a sharecropper, I didn't live in town. I lived out on the farm, seven miles out of town on the Bolandville Plantation. But, during picking time, my best buddy, Red Conner, and I got to go to town on Saturday nights, and we'd go to the Strand to take in a "cowboy pitcher." We loved that, but what we loved even more were the sights we'd see in the back alley of Main Street after the movie. Just down the street from the Strand was the most notorious establishment in Lepanto: Punkin's Pool Hall. On Saturday nights in the fall, Punkin's was a happening place. Of course, we weren't allowed inside those swinging doors, and we would have been too scared to go in if we had been. That didn't matter though, because all the excitement took place in the alley in back of the pool hall. So, as soon as we'd get out of the theater, we'd head for Punkin Alley.

Back in the 1950s, before the time of the automated cotton picker, all the cotton had to be picked by hand. In order to get the cotton picked, the big farmers would bring in Mexicans to help out. The "wetbacks," as they were called, could flat out pick that cotton.

54

Among the sharecroppers, the man who could pick 300 pounds of cotton a day was a wonder. For a wetback, if he didn't have 300 by noon, he would be the laughingstock of his friends. Well, they knew how to make the money, and they knew how to spend it. Picking ended each week for everybody at noon on Saturday, and everyone headed for town. The wetbacks and the sharecroppers, my daddy included, would head for Punkin's and drink Pabst Blue Ribbon beer while their wives, my mama included, brought a few groceries down at Guy Martin's Grocery Store and shopped in E.A. Murphy's Dry Goods Store for cloth and such to make themselves and their daughters' dresses. The kids, Red and I included, would head for the Strand.

By the time the movie had ended, those wetbacks would be pretty well tanked up, and they would be ready for a brawl. Sometimes they would fight one another. Sometimes the fight would be with a sharecropper. But almost every Saturday night, there would be some sort of fight. Punkin Craven wouldn't allow any fighting in his establishment. He would always bellow out, loud enough to be heard from the alley, "Take it outside, boys!" or "Tómelo afuera, los muchachos!" or in both languages if need be. And neither the croppers nor the wetbacks wanted to mess with Punkin, so when he bellowed out those faithful words, Red and I would know what was going to happen next. As Red would always say, "There's fixin' to be a fight." We always had a grand location, up close, standing one on either side of Punkin's back porch. If things got too rough, we could dart out and scamper up the alley and to safety.

Uncle Jack worked on the police force during peak times, like in the fall of the year. Almost always, when the fight started, he would be the first cop to show up. He never waited for backup either. He'd just wade through the crowd, carrying a wooden stick about three feet long and about two inches in diameter. He called this stick his "head-knocker." He'd give a warning, wait a second, and then wade in. By the time the regular deputy, Luther Maynard, got there, both of the culprits would be lying on the sidewalk, nursing their heads and arms. Luther and Jack would drag them off by their shirt collars and lock them up in the city jail. Jack would always yell back as he dragged his victim away, "Break it up, folks. The fight's over." Red, always craving center stage, would say something like, "Hey folks, that's Clyde here's Uncle Jack that done that! And Clyde's a friend of mine." Red and every other boy in that alley would wish that Jack were an uncle of theirs.

On one such occasion, Jack was wading through the crowd to stop a fight between a big old sharecropper and a Mexican. When Jack yelled out, "Now, hold up there, boys," the big old sharecropper replied, "You keep out of this, law dog."

"I'll *law dog* you, you slack-jawed bastard!"

And then Jack stepped up and law dogged the big fellow right across the forehead with the head-knocker. The sharecropper went down like a car had been dropped on his head.

Every fall, a carnival would come to Lepanto. The old city park would be transformed overnight into a most enchanting place. There was carnival food galore: corn dogs, funnel cakes, sno-cones, popcorn, everything imaginable. And then there were the rides, all horribly scary, terribly dangerous, and altogether irresistible. For the men, there would be the hoochy-coochy tent where mysterious-looking, make-up-caked women would dance butt naked on the stage. Then there were the games of chance. One of the games was the one where the customer tries to bust balloons with darts. It cost a whole dollar just for three tries. If a fellow busted one balloon, he got a little seashell ashtray. If he busted two, he got a little velvet picture of this black guy playing a trumpet. If he busted a balloon all three times, he got his choice from an array of huge, brightly colored and beautiful stuffed animals. But a dollar was a hunk of money in those days. A dollar was fifty pounds of cotton—picked, toted, and weighed. A many a dollar was lost on that game of chance, though, and the fellow running the con was making a wad of money. Red and I stood for a long time watching young bucks give it their best try, hoping to win one of those stuffed animals for their admiring girlfriends, but to no avail. Nobody could hit those damn balloons. Red, always the thinker, decided the game was rigged somehow.

"Maybe them's weighted dart heads or something," Red surmised. "After all, that feller running the game is a Yankee. What do you expect?"

Then Uncle Jack showed up. Jack wasn't on duty that night. He was just there, like everyone else, taking in the sights. Red and I were about to get bored with this game and go off on other adventures when we heard someone in the crowd holler, "There's Jack Mize! I'll bet he can bust them damn balloons!"

Well, bust them, he did. The prize he picked was a huge red and white teddy bear. He saw me in the crowd and made me a gift of that bear. The he put up another dollar and won a pink one for Red. Jack was about to walk away, but the crowd wouldn't let him. Everybody was holding dollar bills out to him and saying, "Here, Jack, win me one!"

After giving up about seven or eight grand prizes, the Yankee told Jack that that would be enough for him. Jack had a whole handful of dollar bills, and he shook them in the Yankee fellow's face and said, "My dollars is as good as anybody else's, ain't they?"

The Yankee, not knowing who Jack Mize was, of course, said, "Well, that may be, but you ain't playing no more, Lum!"

"I'll *lum* you, you carpet-bagging bastard!" bellowed Jack, and he fairly clobbered the man up side the head with heel of his hand.

The Yankee staggered backwards, pulled up his pants, and said, "Well, Lum, you just bought your dinner, and I'm gonna feed it to you. I may just give you a double helping." He charged forward and ran square into Jack's fist. The fight went on for fifteen minutes. What the whole affair amounted to, more or less, was the Yankee fellow running toward Jack with his head down, like a football player, and Jack socking him on the top of his head with his fist. Then Jack would step aside and let the fellow pass. The Yankee would shake his head real fast and hard, like he was addled, and then he'd duck his head down again and come a roaring back for more. A fellow can take that kind of treatment for just so long and no longer. Fifteen minutes of it was a god's plenty for the Yankee fellow, so he finally told Jack, "Throw as many of them darts as you have money to pay for."

Now that's what it means to lum a fellow. It's an entertaining sight to watch. And the lumee is going to have a few knots on his head when the lumming is done with. That Yankee was a bumpy mess when Uncle Jack got done with him, I'll have to say it.

Not long after the lumming incident, Uncle Jack got mad at his landlord about his crop settlement. I don't know all the details because I wasn't there, but I heard later that Jack yelled out, "I'll *seed bill* you, you double-dealin' bastard!" Then Jack whipped his landlord's ass and moved to Dundee, Mississippi, that next week. I happened to see Uncle Jack's landlord a few days later at the gin and that seed billing must have been a hell of an experience for him. He was a bruised-up mess.

In his new home in Mississippi, Jack became a sort of farm overseer on a large plantation. He also became an auxiliary deputy for the Tunica County Sheriff's Department. I didn't see much of him after that. He only came back to Arkansas on holidays. In spite of that, his legend lived on in Lepanto, and I was still pretty cocky about his being my uncle.

The years sped along. I grew up, and Uncle Jack grew old. He had a severe stroke at 80 that left him partially paralyzed. He also developed Alzheimer's disease. (Of course, we didn't know that then because we had never heard of such. I just figured all that out recently.) He lost all those bulging muscles, the gamecock walk, and much of that quickness of wit. However, he retained some part of the younger Jack Mize, a part that almost proved to be his undoing.

Aunt Myrtle called me one Saturday afternoon. She started the conversation just this way—"If you don't want your Uncle Jack to go to jail, you'd better come get him, take him home with you, and keep him for a few days." I couldn't get any details out of her over the phone.

"It's a long story," she said. "I'll tell you when you get here. Hurry!" So, I did.

When I drove into the driveway, Aunt Myrtle came out to fill me in. Uncle Jack was standing on the porch of their house trailer, scowling.

"To make a long story short," Myrtle said, "he's done beat hell out of our preacher."

In his latter years, Uncle Jack had gotten religion. Aunt Myrtle, after decades of begging, had finally gotten him to attend the local Baptist church with her. Jack got saved and baptized and became, within a year, one of the deacons of the church. I didn't know about any of this until that day. I was pretty surprised, but that discussion would have to wait for another day. I had to take care of the business at hand.

"Why did he beat up the preacher?" I asked.

"Well, he's a new preacher, right out of seminary. He ain't but about thirty. About a month ago, when he first come, we had a sanging and dinner on the ground, kindly a welcoming party for him. I baked two dewberry cobblers, one for the dinner and one for him to take home with him. That night, after service, he was at the back door, shaking hands with everybody as they went out. When me and Jack got there to shake hands with him, he hugged me and gave me a little ol' peck on the cheek and thanked me for the cobbler. That pissed your Uncle Jack off real bad. You know how he is. Well, he wouldn't even shake hands with the man. And when we got home, he commenced to giving me all kinds of hell. He had me and that preacher having an affair behind his back. And him thirty years old and me seventy. Now, don't that beat everthang? He threatened to beat hell out of the both of us. And he's been mad at me ever since. He won't even eat my cooking nor nothing. Won't speak a word to me. Sleeps in the back bedroom. Won't go near the church. It's been hell on this earth, just trying to live with him for the past month. I been going to church ever Sunday, making excuses for him, a saying he weren't feeling good, telling a lie right there in the Lord's house. Well, last Sunday night, after service, Brother Lewis asked me about Jack again, and I just broke down to crying right there in front of everbody. I told him the whole story, about how Jack's been a doing and what he's been a thinking. Well, Brother Lewis just patted me on the shoulder and said he'd talk to Jack. So, this morning, he come. He knocked on the door, and I was in the back doing some washing. Jack went to the door. He never even asked the man in nor nothing. I was coming up from the back about that time, and I heared Jack ask him, 'What you doing here, preacher man?' And Brother Lewis asks, 'Aren't you going invite me in, Brother Jack?' And Jack says, 'Why, sos you can hump my wife some more?' I could have died right there."

About that time, Uncle Jack interrupted her tale by yelling from the porch. "Boy, are you gonna stand out there and talk to that lying whore, or are you gonna come in here and talk to your Uncle Jack!"

"Hold on just a minute, Uncle Jack. I am coming."

She went on with her tale.

"Well, then the preacher reached up and pinched Jack on the nose and said, 'Now, Brother Jack, you had better behave yourself.' Well, I don't need to tell you how that nose pinching set with Jack. He said, 'I'll *brother* you.' Then, he takened his cane and brought it up right into Brother Lewis' straddle, hard as he could. Then he pulled it back and put the tip of that cane right on the man's forehead and shoved him right off that porch backards. I was a-heading for 'em as quick as I could, but I was too late. I was too slow. I didn't get to see what all happened out here on the porch. They was some scuffling and then a *kerblunk*. I don't know whether Jack fell off the porch on him or if he jumped off on him, but when I got out here, Jack was on top of him, on the ground, a choking him with his cane. Sister Lewis had been waiting in the car, and she had come a running when she seen her husband tumbling off the porch. It takened the both of us to pull Jack off of poor Brother Lewis. Well, she taken him on out of here while I held Jack off. You can see here on my arms where he whacked me with that cane, trying to get past me and get at the preacher. Well, off they went to the hospital. And that is when I called you. I ain't heared nothing from them yet, but I been expecting the law to drive up any minute now."

"I'm counting to three, and when I get done, if you still talking to that whore, I'm going in the house and I'm gonna lock the door behind me! I'll barricade myself up in here and both of you and that preacher and the law can all go to hell as for as I'm concerned."

So, Uncle Jack had brothered the preacher, just like he had lummed that Yankee fellow at the carnival so many years ago. I'll have to admit, even with the situation as serious as it was, I found it awfully hard not to grin just thinking about it. But I knew better than to let Aunt Myrtle see me grin. She was just about as tough as Jack and always had been. I didn't want to tangle with her; that's for sure.

I took Uncle Jack back to Arkansas with me, hoping that a couple of weeks away from home would help him to get his bearings. Those two weeks turned out to be pretty hellish for me. For the first day or two, Jack was totally consumed with his hate for the preacher and his "whore" wife. He told me the whole story, blow by blow, about eleven hundred times. I sat and listened patiently each time, just as if it were today's news. I made few comments. By the third day, I was slipping into some sort of funky-assed depression. I decided that we needed to get out of the house for a while, so I took Jack around to visit with some of his old friends. I thought this would help get his mind going in some other direction. I was wrong. No matter where I took him, the poor soul with whom we were visiting had to listen to the same story a few times. It was interesting to watch their reactions. During the first telling, I could see in their faces that they realized that Jack was having a little problem dealing with reality. I could always see a little twinkle of amusement in their eyes during the part where Jack whipped the preacher's ass. But that amusement didn't last long. During the second and third telling, the hosts would glance over at me with a look that said, "Please, help me." So, I would get Jack up and out of there, and we would go seek out another victim. It was a long two weeks.

Things finally broke. I came home one Friday afternoon to find Jack standing in the middle of my den, crying like a baby.

"I've made a fool out of myself," he said. "You should have told me."

I don't really understand enough about the workings of the human mind to explain it, but he apparently had had a moment of clarity. I was glad, real glad. He told me that, since Mothers' Day was the coming up on Sunday, he wanted me to go to the flower shop and get a dozen roses. The plan was that I take him to the church on Mothers' Day, and at precisely 11:00 o'clock, between Sunday school and the song service, he would present the roses to Myrtle in front of the entire church. It sounded like a fine plan to me.

We had a flat tire on the way to the church. This upset Uncle Jack. He began to backslide. He suspected that the flat tire might be a sign. Perhaps he had been right to begin with. Perhaps the preacher was poking that whore after all. I tried to calm him down. I soon gave up on that and concentrated on hurrying up with that tire change.

When we arrived at the church, the song service had already begun. Well, so much for the grand presentation. The whole congregation was standing, singing "When the Roll is Called Up Yonder." We found Aunt Myrtle where we both knew she would be — in the Mize pew. He got on one side of her and I on the other. He handed her the roses. Every eye in the church was upon them. It was a touching moment. Aunt Myrtle cried. Uncle Jack cried. I cried. Everybody cried. By the end of the song, I could hear people sobbing all over the auditorium.

After the song, the congregation sat down, and the preacher got up to make the weekly announcements and to welcome the visitors. I had never met the man. He had been sitting behind the pulpit during the singing, so this was my first chance to see him. He was a short, chubby fellow, young, but as bald as a jug. I don't think he had much of a neck, but I couldn't tell for sure because he had on a neck brace. He also had two black eyes and eight scab-covered, parallel scratches starting at the top of his head and coming down to midway of his large forehead. The scratches were perfectly aligned. They looked like bedded-up rows in a cotton field, straight ones, ones that a fellow would be proud to have planted. To be honest, that preacher's appearance would have made a cat laugh, and you know yourself that it's real hard to get a cat to laugh. So, what happened next was not my fault. One minute I'm just sitting there crying about those roses, and the next, I look up and see that preacher and a laugh bursts out of me, totally unexpected. Aunt Myrtle elbowed me really hard, and I looked down at the floor and tried to stop laughing. It took a good deal of time. Aunt Myrtle was elbowing me the whole time, too.

Finally, I got a hold of myself and thought everything was going to be ok. But I knew not to look toward the pulpit again. So, my intention was to just look up there in the general direction, but not directly at the preacher himself. Well, you know how it always is. When a fellow tells himself not to look at a thing, he can't keep from looking at it, no way in the world. And, when I did, I busted out again. Aunt Myrtle was about to beat me to death. Then Jack got tickled at me, and he started laughing. The fellow behind us commenced to laughing, and then the thing just spread out all around. That poor preacher didn't have a clue what was going on. He was right in the middle of reading off a prayer list, and the people were trying to stifle their laughter. It was a mighty inopportune time for folks to be acting that way, and I guess that everybody else realized that about the time that I did and felt ashamed. The laughter began to die down. The preacher, meanwhile, had stopped mid-sentence and glared in silence at his congregation. When the laughter had completely stopped, he let the dead silence hover over us for what seemed like ten or twelve minutes, but it might not have been that long, and then he said, "Let us bow our heads."

I was so glad of that. It would give me a chance to get myself under control a little better.

The preacher began his prayer.

"Our Blessed Father, we thank thee for the joy of the blessings which we so often take for granted. We pause now to think of those who could not be with us today to share our joy. We pray for the blind, and the lame, and the halt, and for others not so fortunate."

Now, is it just me? Am I such a bad person? Wouldn't you have laughed at that—the "others not so fortunate" part? I think you would have. I couldn't any more help it than the man in the moon. And neither could Uncle Jack. It just wasn't our fault at all.

Well, we finally calmed down again and Aunt Myrtle let up on us with those elbows, and the preacher set in and preached the longest, most boring sermon in the history of Christianity. I looked at the floor the whole time and kept quiet, as best I could. So did Jack. We tried not to look at the preacher or at one another. We were successful at the former, but less successful at the latter. A couple of times, our eyes met and we busted out. Aunt Myrtle beat on us some more with those elbows of hers. But, finally, it was over. During the closing prayer, the preacher tippy-toed his way up the aisle toward the doorway so he could shake hands with everybody as they left. Jack and I went out the side door and tried to make it to the car. It didn't work though.

"Jack, you come up here right now!" shouted Aunt Myrtle. "Ain't you got something you wanna say to Brother Lewis?" She was standing in the doorway, and the preacher was there beside her, glaring at both of us, as was the entire congregation.

I hung back at the car. Poor Uncle Jack went on up, meek as a mouse, and I watched as he shook hands with the preacher and said something to him. The preacher responded, and they hugged each other. Uncle Jack was a little misty-eyed when he walked out to the car.

"I'll ride on home with Myrtle. You just foller us and have dinner with us before you go back."

I thanked him, but begged off, claiming that I really needed to be heading back. I hugged my old uncle and asked him if he thought he was going to be all right now.

"I will be, so long as that preacher man don't try to pinch my nose again," he said with a twinkle in his eye.

As I drove home, I thought of the two-week ordeal I had been through, and I thought back to my childhood and to the young and robust Jack Mize, of whom I had always been so fond and so proud. I also thought of Hamlet's "O, what a rogue and peasant slave am I" soliloquy in which he says, "Who calls me villain? Breaks my pate across? Tweaks me by the nose?" Hamlet decided that he "should take it" and that he was "pigeon-livered" and lacked "gall."

*Well*, I thought as I drove toward Memphis, *my Uncle Jack never did lack for gall; that's for sure.* I smiled as I thought of the preacher, the painful scratches on his head, his raccoon eyes, and his fat neck bound up in that brace. If he had only known the Jack Mize that I had known, he would have known better. He'd have never tweaked Jack's nose. He would have probably gotten his ass whipped anyway, though, since Jack thought the preacher was messing with his wife. But, at least, had that been the cause of the ass whipping, the preacher could have put it all off on Jack and his mental condition. He wouldn't have to spend the rest of his days thinking, "Man, I wish I hadn't tweaked Jack Mize's nose."

Uncle Jack didn't live long after that incident. I got the call from Aunt Myrtle about two months later, telling me that Jack had passed. Brother Lewis did a fine job on the funeral sermon. There was, of course, no mention of their former troubles. He praised him for his life's work as a farmer and a police officer and for his latter-day duties as a deacon in the church. After the service, as I passed by the casket to take a last look at that old familiar face, I wept at the loss of something, something more than just the loss of a dear uncle. Something else, I felt, had passed too. But I can't, to this day, find the words to express what it is exactly, so I'll just close with that.

# The Hero in My House

In the spring of 2004, I got acquainted with John H. Briggs, Jr. John is a farmer who lives in Reydell, Arkansas, about a 2½ hour drive from my home in Crawfordsville, Arkansas. John graduated from Crawfordsville High School in 1942. When I first met him, I noticed that the license plate on his Ford pickup said "POW."

I am an English instructor at East Arkansas Community College in Forrest City, Arkansas. I chose English as my major because in college I discovered a love for writing and for literature. I made my love my life's work. But a close runner-up to my interest in English would be my love for American history. The American Civil War and World War II have been topics on the top of my reading list all of my life. When I saw that license plate, my interest piqued.

"Was John a POW?" I asked a long-time friend of John's.

"Yes, he was," she replied.

"In World War II?"

"Yes."

"Do you think he would want to talk about it?"

"I don't know," she said. "He's never mentioned it to me except to say that he attends reunions with other POWs."

My experience has been that World War II veterans are sometimes reluctant to talk about the war. My late father-in-law, Frank Alpe, is a case in point. I had known him for years and had often tried to strike up a conversation with him about his war experiences, but he wouldn't have much to say. Then one day we were working together on a little carpentry project and, for some strange reason, he began to talk. It turned out that he was in the Navy and that he had piloted one of the landing crafts that took those brave boys onto Omaha Beach on D-Day. I never looked at my father-in-law quite the same after that day. I had always liked him. I had liked him a lot, in fact, but from that day until the day that they blew taps over his grave, I looked at him with something akin to worship. *There he is*, I thought as we would sit at Frank's breakfast room table. *He's one of 'Those Boys of D-Day.'*

Now I had another golden opportunity. I had the chance to actually talk to a POW from World War II. I knew that I must approach him carefully or I might never get him to tell me anything. *I'll try to get to know him first*, I thought, *and work my way into an interview with him about his experiences in the war*. Well, as it turned out, John H. Briggs, Jr., was one of the easiest men in the world to get to know. A nicer, friendlier, more humble man I have never met. He soon invited my wife and me to his home in Reydell. He took us into his home and made us feel so welcome that I felt as if we had been long-time friends. Before the night was over, I asked him about the license plate.

"Yes," he said. "We were shot down over Romania in April of '44. Our mission was to bomb the Polesti oil fields."

Just that bit of information was enough to make my jaw drop and my brain to go soft for a second. The very next words out of my mouth were, "I can't believe I'm talking to a POW, a hero of World War II."

John was quick to correct me. "I was no hero," he said. "I just did my duty like a lot of other boys, and some of them didn't come back. Those boys were the heroes."

As he said that, I sensed a change in John. I saw a sadness in his eyes, and I heard a break in his voice. I knew that I had touched a delicate chord within him. I knew that my questions had made him feel the sting of painful memories, memories of friends long lost but still remembered, and of grief unspeakable.

We spent the night at John's house, and the next day he showed me a documentary film about the bombing of the Polesti oil fields. John was actually in the film in a scene shot on the day that the POWs were rescued. I didn't press John that day for more details about his capture or his imprisonment, and he didn't volunteer much. I knew that I shouldn't press my luck.

I knew that John came to Crawfordville quite often to visit old friends. The drive is long and would pretty much wear him out. Before we left to come home, I told John that when he came again to Crawfordsville, he could come to my house to rest. I told him I would have him a key made so that he could just come on in and make himself at home if we were still at work He was grateful and agreed to accept the invitation. When I got home, I had him a key made. Meanwhile, I started planning for his visit. I had decided that I wanted to write John's story. But I knew that I would have to be careful about how I approached him or he might shy away from me. His modesty could very well nip my plan in the bud. That, I felt, would be a great tragedy, not just because I wouldn't get to write it, but because the story could be lost forever. When John did come, he spent the night at our house. Before we went to bed, I began asking him questions about his war experiences. We talked for several hours. The next morning, I left him the following note on the breakfast room table.

Dear John,

I want you to know what an honor it has been to have you as a guest in our home. Listening to the story of your wartime experiences has been like walking back in time to those difficult days for our country. This story needs to be told if for no other reason than that generations of Americans not yet born must know and never forget the sacrifices that were made by young boys like yourself. You and your generation paid the price for the freedoms we sometimes take for granted. Some paid the ultimate price, and your story will honor them as well.

When you come to this part of the country, our door is always open to you. Please consider this place your home away from home.

Respectfully,
Clyde and Angela

Here is John's story.

In the spring of 1942, John H. Briggs, Jr., graduated from Crawfordsville High School, and the future for him looked extremely bright. John was quite a baseball player, and the scouts had been around. Upon graduation, he got the call from the St. Louis organization right away. He was off to Houston for baseball camp. John loved the game of baseball, so this was a dream come true. Only two months into training, however, John got yet another call. This time the call was in the form of a draft notice. He had been called up to serve his country in her hour of need. He admits that he was disappointed about his baseball career, but he understood what his first duty was. After he reported for duty, the Army became interested in John's baseball playing ability and offered him a chance to avoid going to war. He could play ball for the U.S. Army instead. John turned down the offer. If he was going to be "in it" he wanted to be "in it" all the way.

After several months of training, John was assigned to the 450th Bomber Group as a tail gunner on a bomber. He flew on thirty-nine missions over Italy and Northern Africa before his crew became a part of the attack force sent to take out the Polesti oil fields in Romania. This target was important to the Allied war effort because these oil fields supplied Germany with a fourth of its oil. The fields simply had to be shut down so that the advancing Nazi war machine would grind to a halt.

On April 16, 1944, John's crew was leading a raid when they were crippled by enemy fire. The bomber's wing was damaged and its fuel tank was hit. The other planes in the group pulled on ahead, and John and his fellow crewmen were left alone to face the fighters of the German Luftwaffe. Like lions after a wounded antelope, the fighters closed in, firing away at the injured aircraft. John and his fellow gunners fought back as best they could. Before long, two of the gunners were killed and the radioman, Dale Swift, was severely wounded. The German fighters pursued as long as their fuel allowance would permit and then they dropped back. The object now was to get back to safe territory before the plane ran out of fuel. That was not to be. The word came to bail out. John helped Swift into his parachute and they jumped.

On the way down, John could see the locals coming from all directions, some carrying antique rifles, some carrying pitchforks. I asked John how he felt when he saw those people gathering on the ground with their weapons, and he admitted that it was "pretty scary." He had heard stories about American pilots who had been shot down over Germany. Some of them were killed by the locals.

Many times, on the other hand, the American pilots would be protected by the very German pilots who had shot them down. There was a code of honor between these fighting men, enemies though they may have been. John and Swift were now prisoners of war, and luckily, the Romanian locals treated them decently after all.

They were loaded onto a horse-drawn cart, taken to the nearest town, and locked up in the local jail. Within a few days, all the survivors of John's crew had been rounded up and were brought to the jail. Then they were sent to Bucharest, where they would spend the next several months in a Romanian prisoner of war camp.

Life in the camp was bleak, but their captors treated them pretty well. The food was so bad that boiled potato peels were considered a delicacy. The Romanian guards were decent, but on occasion, members of the German S.S. would come by to inspect the camp. In John's words, "When those fellows came around, you had better stay out of their way if you could, because they just had to kick you if they got close enough."

One of John's fellow prisoners, Kenny Kenosegher, could speak fluent German. To pass the time, John, Kenosegher, and James Bennett planned a daring escape. I'm not sure how elaborate the plan was, and John was too modest to go into much detail. But, as John put it, "We just walked up to the front gate and Kenny said something to them in German and the door swung open." They were out only three days, living off carrots they managed to steal out of gardens and sleeping on haystacks at night. When they were recaptured, they were "treated kinda bad for a while." They were thrown into the hole and given only bread and water as punishment for escaping. This was in addition to "a little kicking around" that they got for the trouble they had caused. As John told me about the daring escape, he seemed almost embarrassed to tell it. But, as I listened, I remembered having heard at some time in the past, perhaps in a movie, that the P.O.W.'s first duty is to try to escape. How easy it might have been to just "sit out the war." But these brave men saw their chance and they took it.

When Romania capitulated to the Russians, John and his fellow prisoners were set free by the Romanians. The prison gates were opened, but the Americans were on their own and unarmed. The battle was on in Bucharest between the Russians and the Germans, and Allied bombers were hitting targets all around, including the prison camp itself. John and some of his friends dug a large foxhole in the compound and hunkered down for a few days, until the bombing subsided. Then the announcement was made that a daring rescue was coming. In spite of the fact that the battle for Bucharest was still raging, American planes were going to come in and take the prisoners out. And take them out they did. On the appointed day, they assembled at the airport and were rescued.

Being the first prisoners of World War II to be freed, John and his friends were treated to a hero's welcome. Their ordeal was finally over. John wasn't sent on any more missions after that. The war soon ended and all the boys, or at least all those who had survived, were sent home.

John came home to Crawfordsville unexpectedly. How I would have loved to have been there and to have seen his mother's face when she looked up and saw her boy coming in the door.

When John H. Briggs, Jr., came into my life many years later and became my friend, he was welcomed as a hero once again. Let me explain why. When I was a child, I became a Civil War fanatic. I loved to read about the brave boys on both sides of that tragic conflict. I remember one evening hearing on the radio that the last Civil War veteran had died. That night, I lay in my bed and cried at his passing. I felt that I had, in some strange way, been cheated. I had loved those "Boys of the Blue and the Grey" so much, and I had been born too late to know them. And now they were all gone forever. I felt that with the death of the last one, we, as a country (and I, personally), had lost something of great importance.

Many years have passed since I wept for that last old rebel. I, myself, am now getting old. But these GIs of WWII are older still, and their ranks are growing thinner and thinner with each passing year. This is why I welcome John as a hero in my home. I am proud to have been allowed the privilege of knowing John Briggs personally. I am grateful to him; and to my father-in-law, Frank Alpe; and to all those brave boys and girls, living and dead, who put everything on the line for their country in World War II. For them, duty, honor, and country were more important than life itself. Every American owes them a huge debt. We should all honor them while we still have the opportunity.

# A Dying Grace

When Angela and I married, I found out right away that I had some interesting in-laws. A good case in point is her Uncle Vince and Aunt Gloria Plumbo. They were in their late sixties at the time and were already retired. Gloria had been a nurse, and Vince had done various things in his life.

He was originally from Minnesota. He had met Gloria in the 1950s when he was playing professional baseball for the Memphis Chicks. He was a catcher. His den was a museum of sorts. He had pictures on the walls of himself behind the plate. He had baseballs signed by some of the really notables. I love the game of baseball, and that memorabilia sparked my interest and drew me to Vince. A stronger draw, however, was the man's personality. Vince was no ordinary guy.

One thing that I found unusual about him was that he was a man with a thousand questions. No matter what tale I might be telling (I love to tell tales), Vince not only seemed interested, but he also wanted to know all the details. If I were talking about my job as a teacher or some incident that had happened in class, he wanted to know all the details. He would ask a million questions. I used to think of it in this way—he was like an artist. I was the holder of the paint. He would ask questions as a painter might reach out for different shades of color. He would take whatever story I was telling him and paint a picture of it in his mind, one that he could go back to later, in solitude, and ponder. This in Vince may have been an irritating trait to some, but it was fascinating to me. Maybe it was the teacher in me, but I always found it refreshing that he cared enough about what I had to say to go to all that trouble. He made me feel as if what I had to say really mattered.

Another thing that I liked about the man was that he always seemed to be glad to see me. That may seem like a small thing to some, but it's a big thing to me. Whenever we met up, at his house, at my house, or at any other place, Vince would grin big and take my hand and give it a hardy shake. All of this endeared him to me. I simply liked Vince Plumbo and valued his friendship.

Vince was Italian. His family was from the south end of the boot. Gloria's family was from the center, around Ancona. A few years ago, my wife and I went to visit her relatives there. We asked Aunt Gloria to go. It was the dream of her life to go there. We asked Vince to go too, but he declined. But, after all the questions he asked about the trip, before and after, he wound up experiencing a good bit of Italy after all.

Gloria died shortly after our trip. She battled cancer for over a year. Vince was a tender caregiver, waiting on her every need. He had fallen in love with her when she came to watch him play baseball, and he loved her for the rest of her life. He and Gloria only had one child, Anntonia. She lives only a few miles from Vince in the city of West Memphis. Her husband, Pat Mcgruder, is an architect. They have two sons, Austin and Grayson. Anntonia (Antzee) was the apple of Vince's eye. The Plumbo home was a shrine to her. Her childhood pictures were everywhere. His two grandsons were his life. He always had time for them and taught them the best way to hold a baseball bat.

Last year, Vince was diagnosed with cancer. It was the fast-acting kind, he was told. He went through the chemotherapy and radiation and that bought him some time, but after that, the cancer showed up again. His doctor tried to get him to go through another round of radiation, but he also told him that it would only prolong the inevitable. Vince decided to forego that option and accept his fate.

It was a pretty sad night, that Sunday night when Angela and I went by to talk to Vince about his decision. Angela is a nurse, and Vince began to ask her a ton of questions about what he could expect in the days to come. Typical of Vince, he wanted details. Angela tried to answer any questions she could, but she wound up telling him that she would set him up with an appointment with the doctor she works for, Dr. Robert Kulinski. Vince was happy about that and told her to set it all up. Then the conversation took a turn, and it became one of the most memorable conversations I have ever had with anyone—anywhere—anytime.

I should tell you here that Vince was a devout Catholic. He began to talk to us about his feelings about his impending death. The conversation went like this:

He said, "Well, I'm eighty-two years old. I've had a good life. I'm not bitter about this. I'm not trying to sound brave or anything, but I am ready to die, if I must die. I don't want to suffer. Nobody would. But I accept it. And I have made my peace with God about it. You know, Clyde, we Catholics believe in what's called a dying grace. God gives it to us when our time comes around. I prayed and asked him to give me a dying grace, and I know that he has. I am at peace. I just hope it comes quickly. It will be too hard on Antzee and the boys if it drags out too long."

I said, "Well, Vince, when the time comes that you need someone to stay with you, you know that Angela and I will be here with you. Antzee will be with you during the day, and we will come to be with you at night."

"That's good to know," he said. "I appreciate that. Maybe it won't drag on too long. I hate to be such a bother to everyone."

"It won't be a bother, my friend. It will be an honor," I said, and I really meant that from the heart.

Dr. Kulinski met with Vince for over an hour. Vince, of course, asked a thousand questions, and Dr. Kulinski was gracious beyond belief. He told him the straight truth as well as he could about what was likely to happen to Vince in the days ahead. He assured him that he could prescribe drugs that would keep him from suffering. He assured him that it would not be long. A couple of times during the conversation, the good doctor let a tear escape. I am sure that Vince noticed and appreciated the doctor's compassion. There are lots of folks with the degree hanging on the wall, but true doctors are a little scarcer. Dr. Robert Kulinski is a prince of a man and the finest of doctors. Vince was grateful to him for his candor and kindness.

Vince wanted to be private in his suffering. He had Antzee bring the boys by a few days after his visit with the doctor. He wanted to tell them goodbye. He didn't want them to see him after that. I cried a lot that day, thinking about that sad goodbye scene.

To honor Vince's privacy, I won't go into detail about Vince's decline. I will say this, however. In the first week, any time I came into his room, Vince would be holding his rosary beads. He was always appreciative that I had come by. Then the day came, as we all knew it would, that Vince could not get out of bed. Angela and I would go to Vince's after work and she would spend the night. Vince's sister, Margaret, came from Minnesota to be with him. The affection between the two of them was very evident. In the days ahead, I would get to know Margaret. She, like her brother, is a fine person. I felt a bond with her immediately. I told her one day that she was a wonderful sister to Vince.

"Not as good as he is," she quickly replied. "He has always been a wonderful brother to me."

One night I noticed that Vince's rosary beads were in the nightstand. By then he was in and out of consciousness. I realized that he could no longer pray as he had been doing. Now I'm not Catholic, and some of my Baptist brethren might think I should be strung up for this, but from that day until the day he died, I said ten "Hail Marys" for my friend every day, and I am glad that I did. Otherwise, all I have to say about the death of Vince Plumbo is that he died with courage and with dignity. I was proud of him.

I read somewhere that some doctors have done research on the phenomenon called "the near-death experience." They say that a goodly number of those people come away from the experience changed in many ways. For one thing, almost all of them come away from it believing that the two most important things about life on this earth are that we treat one another kindly and that we learn all we can while we are here. Well, Vince didn't have to "see the tunnel" to learn those simple truths. He spent his life in a quest to learn lots of things, to find out the specifics, to look at things closely. He also knew how to treat his fellowman. He was a kind and gracious man and a good friend. I will never forget him.

# The Merry-Go-Round

When my grandson, Courtney Allen Rodgers, was born, my daughter, Angie, had had a long, drawn-out labor. As a result, when the doctor came to tell me that I could see the baby, he warned me that the baby's head would look "a little pointed."

"Will it stay that way?" I asked as we were walking down the hall toward the nursery.

"No," the doctor said assuringly. "He'll be as normal as can be in a day or two."

I was relieved. I had been a nervous wreck all that morning. This was my first grandchild, and I wanted everything to be perfect.

When I got to the nursery, the nurse behind the glass picked up my grandson and brought him over to the glass so I could see him better. He had a little knit cap on his head. It looked badly pointed.

*It's the cap,* I thought. *I know his head isn't THAT pointed!*

I motioned to the nurse to take the cap off his head. She gave me a look that said she didn't think that would be a good idea. I gave her a look that said, "Take the damn thing off!"

She took it off.

I almost fainted. His little head looked like it had been in a pencil sharpener!

"Doc, are you telling me that his head is going to be normal in a few days? I find that hard to believe."

"Now, Mr. Rodgers, you're a teacher. Have you ever had a student with a head that pointed?"

"Yes. Charles Conway."

"Now, Mr. Rodgers, was Charles Conway's head THAT pointed?"

"Yes, sir, THAT pointed."

Now, Charles was a little kid I taught in my very first year as a teacher and he was a pure cone-head.

The doctor assured me, over and over, that Courtney would not be a cone-head. Well, I decided right then and there that I didn't believe a word of it, but that I would love him just the same, cone-head and all.

I'll have to admit that the doctor was right. Unbelievably, within a few days, Court's head was as pretty and round as it could be. (However, I still am not sure it would have been round if I hadn't rubbed on it for hours during each of those days. I shaped his noggin up perfectly and, to this day, when I look at him, I think about how lucky he is to have had me for a grandfather. Not every grandfather would have taken the time and put out all the effort on that head.)

My daughter and Courtney live just around the corner from the school in Lepanto. One day, when Court was twelve years old, they drove by the school and noticed that the old merry-go-round from the playground was out by the trash bin. The school was throwing the thing away. That same old merry-go-round was on that school ground when I was a kid. I was glad when I heard that they had asked permission to take it home with them. They not only saved an old memory for me, but they also had gotten a fine old merry-go-round to boot. Angie planned to set it up in her backyard, but she first wanted to restore it to its former glory. They leaned it up against the back of the house and sanded it and painted it bright orange. It was one of the old type merry-go-rounds, built before plastic had been invented. It was solid steel and weighed a ton. And they had it looking mighty fine.

A few nights later, I was teaching a night class at the college. Someone knocked on my door. When I looked up and saw my wife, Angela, I knew that something was awfully wrong. In seventeen years of marriage, she had never interrupted one of my classes before. Plus, the look on her face told me worlds. Something was bad wrong. I stopped in mid-sentence and went to the door.

"Courtney is on the way to the hospital. That merry-go-round fell on his head and he's hurt really bad," Angela said.

I dismissed my class, and we headed to the emergency room. When we got there, they had him on a bed. He was conscious, but his face was black and blue. Worse than that, his whole head looked all warped out of shape. I almost passed out, but when he looked up and said weakly, "Hi, Pappy and Ranny. I'm glad ya'll are here," I knew that I must try to be strong and not let him see how upset I was. To be honest, my heart was breaking.

Later, out in the hall, my daughter told us what had happened. After dinner that evening, Court had asked if he could go next door to play with a friend. Angie told him to go ahead. He went out the backdoor, but decided to climb around on the merry-go-round before he went to see his friend. The merry-go-round, still leaning on the back of the house, had fallen over, right on him, crushing his face. My daughter, thinking he was next door, didn't know that he was in trouble. He somehow managed to lift the thing off his face and get out from under it. Angie looked up when he came in the back door.

"Mama, I need a doctor. Am I gonna die?"

Tears were running down his face. Those were the only tears he shed throughout the whole ordeal. That night in the hospital, he kept assuring me and his Ranny that he was going to be okay, and for us not to worry.

When the x-rays came back, the doctor told us that there were several broken bones, especially the ones around his eyes. He was not sure, because of the swelling, if it would require surgery. It all depended on whether or not the bones of his face were still in place. Nothing could be done until the swelling went down. That took several days.

I have never felt so helpless in my life. I thought of that first day, that day that I saw that pointed head. I thought of my silly attempts at rounding it out. But this was beyond my skills. There wasn't a thing I could do to help him. And as far as just being there for him, he was more "there for me" than I was "there for him."

God is kind and merciful. The bones were still in place and no surgery was needed. He went through months of healing. And a year later, he had to have surgery on his sinuses. He went through that like a trooper, never complaining, never showing fear. He's fine now. His face looks normal. He is a mighty brave little guy, and we are all awfully proud of him.

I have thought often of that pointed head, and I have thought of that awful night and of that warped and bruise face. I wanted so badly to just reach over and rub it back into shape, but I couldn't. I just hope that I can be the kind of Pappy who can help to shape his character by living a life before him that will set him a good example. I certainly don't need to teach him anything about courage. He already knows about that. Somehow, I feel certain that he will do just fine.

# Her Father's Daughter

I was helping my father-in-law, Frank Alpe, convert part of a garage into a dining room for the restaurant next door when we had our most intimate conversation. He owned both businesses and had decided to expand the restaurant and downsize the garage. After he had retired his mechanics position with American Airlines a few years earlier, he had worked on cars in the shop. He was getting older now and had cut back on his work. That day, as we worked at putting a wall between the garage and the new dining room, we talked about various things. He was an interesting man to talk to. The conversation got around to his World War II experiences.

That day I learned that he had been in the Navy during the war. I also learned that he had piloted one of the landing crafts that delivered the soldiers to the beaches at Normandy on D-Day.

"We had our orders," he said. "We had been told to deliver a load of men to the beach and then turn around and go back out to the ship and get another load. We were told that, no matter what, we could not pull anyone out of the water. We couldn't take the time. We had to go get more men. Everything depended on that, we were told. There were wounded men in the water, crying out for help, begging us to stop and pick them up. But we couldn't do it. If we had, there would have been no end to it. There were just so many. I will never forget the sound of the wounded men in the water. I hear their screams sometimes in my sleep."

As he told me this story, I saw that there were tears welling up in his eyes. I wondered how many tears he had shed over the past fifty years for those poor souls. I pitied him for his memories. That story explained a lot to me about this man.

For one thing, it explained to me something about why he was a man so easily moved to tears. I had seen him cry while watching a sad movie many times. I had seen him cry when talking about his uncle whom he described as "a prince of a man." Frank's father had died in an accident when Frank only three years old. Both his parents were Italian immigrants. When Marco Alpe died, he left his widow, Anntonia, with five small children to raise. Frank's Uncle Stanislaus (Uncle Shoe) had come to America to help his sister raise Frank and his siblings. In 1959, on a visit to his home in Montignano, Uncle Shoe died. He had been a father to Frank, and Frank could never speak of Uncle Shoe without weeping. It was in that same year that Frank's second daughter, Angela, was born.

Frank and his wife, Juanita, had a large family. Angela was the fifth of seven children. He loved all his children, but I was able to see, firsthand, the close bond between Frank and Angela. Perhaps it was the close proximity of time between Uncle Shoe's death and Angela's birth that endeared her to him. When Uncle Shoe had left for Italy to spend the summer, he had told Frank that, upon his return, Frank would have another child. He gave the child his blessing in advance. Angela was born that July. Uncle Shoe never got to see her. I have often thought that Frank Alpe transferred some of his love for his uncle to his daughter. He was the kind of man who would make that sort of mystical connection.

Although Angela was twenty-eight years old and had a twelve-year-old daughter when we decided to marry, I formally asked her father for her hand. We were in his pickup, driving around the little town of Crawfordsville. He was touched by the gesture, and he wept. He thanked me and gave us his blessing. I had already grown very fond of Frank by that time, and his blessing meant a lot to me. In the years that followed, the relationship between Angela and Frank would be a subject of great interest and curiosity to me.

Frank was a tall, thin man, and he had a striking resemblance to Gary Cooper. He even wore cowboy boots and western-style clothes. He was a devout Catholic. When he dressed for church, he looked just like the town marshal in the movie *High Noon*. His hair was combed the same way as Cooper's, in fact, and he didn't like to go to the barbershop. He liked for Angela to cut his hair. So, every month or so, Frank would take a seat in the breakfast room of his house and Angela would give him a haircut. Those barbering sessions were special times for me. I loved to watch the two of them interact.

In spite of the fact that Frank had the saddest eyes I had ever seen, he had a keen sense of humor. Frank was never as quick to laugh as he was to cry, so I sure did enjoy watching him get amused. He would grin really big and those sad eyes would lose their sadness for a second and actually twinkle. He always thought I was a funny fellow, I think, and I liked to make him laugh. Those haircutting times were always a good opportunity for me.

One day, as Angela was giving her father a trim, I was perched on a barstool, looking on. He was facing me across the table, and Angela was behind him, cutting his hair.

"Well, did ya'll hear about the excitement in Crawfordsville last night?" he asked.

"No," said Angela. "What happened?"

"Well, the Jacobsons were at it again. The whole bunch was fighting and someone had to call the law. By the time the law got there, all eleven of 'em were out in the yard. They had chosen up sides and were having a free-for-all. The officer had to call in backup to break it all up. There must have been ten police cars in the yard before it was over. They loaded 'em all up and took 'em off the Marion jail."

Angela spoke before she thought. She said, "Well, I hate that I missed that. You know, that's all those Jacobsons know, just fightin' and, ah, ah…that's all they know, just fightin'."

Angela was cutting the back of Frank's hair, and he'd had his head bent over. When she said that, Frank looked up at me without raising his head. He didn't want Angela to know what he was thinking. There was that twinkle in those eyes. Dead silence followed. Angela's slip of the tongue had embarrassed them both. I couldn't resist exploiting the situation.

"Angela," I said, "you were about to say something else. Those Jacobsons don't know anything but fighting and…what else were you about to say?"

If looks could kill, I wouldn't be sitting here writing this story today. She nailed me with her eyes. Meanwhile, Frank was trying his best to show no reaction at all. He was having a hard time of it.

"That's all I was going to say. They just like to fight."

"No, I'm sure that you were about to say something else. I gotta know now. What else is it that the Jacobsons like to do?"

"They don't like to do anything else. They just like to fight. That's all I was going to say," she said with her mouth. *"Shut the hell up, right now!"* she said with her eyes.

Frank tried not to look at me, but he couldn't help himself. His shoulders began to jerk. He wanted to laugh, but was too embarrassed for Angela. I had them both right where I wanted them.

"How many of those Jacobson kids are there? Eleven? It sounds to me like they like to do something else besides fight. What was it you were about to say, anyway?"

It was a still-frame moment. These two were so very close, but at the same time, they were so shy toward each other. Either one of them would have laughed if the other one had not been in the room. But neither would let on as long as the other was present. I found that really fascinating. It was fun as well.

On Thanksgiving morning 1992, the Alpe family had gathered at Frank's for the traditional turkey dinner. Frank checked on the turkey and then went into his bedroom. I was in the den, watching television. When he walked through the room, I saw that something was wrong. I went to check on him and found him leaning on his desk.

"Are you all right, Frank?"

"Get Angela," he said.

Angela took one look at him and knew that something very serious was happening. We called 911. Frank Alpe died that day, shortly after he was brought into the emergency room.

Angela was totally unprepared to give up her daddy. She dropped out of life for a while. She took little interest in anything. She was usually in quiet thought. Sometimes, days would go by without a half dozen words being passed between us. Many times, she would cry uncontrollably, just out of the blue. I didn't know what to do to help her. I suggested that she seek professional help to deal with her grief. She rejected this idea, saying that it wouldn't help.

On Angela's first birthday after Frank's death, I came home to find her sitting in the middle of the living room floor, weeping bitterly. I tried to talk to her or get her to talk to me, but to no avail at first. Finally, she got control of herself enough to say, "Daddy always called me on my birthday. I just miss him so much. I just wish I could hear from him."

Immediately, the telephone rang!

She picked up the phone and said, "Hello?"

There was silence on the line.

She gently placed the phone on the cradle and said, "It was my daddy. He just wished me a happy birthday."

After that day, Angela came back from that far-off place where she had been. That's not to say that the grieving process was over. It never will be, but that is as it should be. But, that day, that phone call did more good for Angela than any counselor or therapy session could ever do. It gave her back her life.

I know that there of those who would dismiss this with a chuckle and say that phones ring all the time. People hang up all the time. Everybody, at one time or another, has answered a ring only to find silence on the line.

Well, all that is true. But no one will ever convince me or Angela that that phone call was just a common occurrence. Since that day, Angela has known that her father is with her always.

On her first trip to Italy, Angela brought back a handful of soil from the cemetery where Frank's Uncle Shoe is buried. Upon her return, she went to Frank's grave and dug a hole. She added the Italian soil to the soil of Arkansas. Frank liked that a lot; I am sure of that.

I don't consider myself a superstitious person. However, I do believe in miracles, and that phone call on Angela's birthday was Frank Alpe saying, "Happy Birthday, Angela. I love you."

Printed in the United States
35096LVS00006B/301-402